WOULD YOU

RATHER FOR KIDS

Christmas Edition

How to Play

Step 1

Split into two teams whether that be boys vs girls, kids vs parents, or any mix of your choice. If possible, also assign one person as a referee.

Step 2

Decide who gets to go first. Which team can do the most pushups? Which team can guess the number between 1 and 10 from someone not playing the game? Or just some good old fashioned rock paper scissors?

Step 3

The starting team has to ask a question from the book and the opposing team has 10 seconds to not only choose an option but to also give a meaningful reason as to why they chose what they did. The referee decides whether the answer is acceptable.

Step 4

The team can discuss their answer together but only one player can give the answer. The person answering has to alternate every turn.

Step 5

If the player who is answering can't choose or give a good reason then that player is out for the game and can't answer anymore or be involved in the team discussion.

Step 6

Repeat until all players are eliminated.

Would you rather...

Laugh HO HO HO as your usual laugh **OR** *have a squeaky voice like an elf?*

Would you rather...

Be the only person that doesn't get a gift **OR** *be the only person that gave a gift?*

Would you rather...

*Never have to pay for clothes again **OR** food?*

Would you rather...

*Celebrate Christmas on a snowy cold day **OR** a warm day without snow?*

Would you rather...

*Go to Disneyworld **OR** Universal Studios*

for a Christmas vacation?

Would you rather...

*Be able to talk with reindeers **OR** speak*

an extra language?

Would you rather...

*Get cash **OR** presents for Christmas?*

Would you rather...

*Have super vision **OR** super hearing as a Christmas wish?*

Would you rather...

Receive an offensive Christmas card from Grandma **OR** give her one?

Would you rather...

Have Rambo **OR** the Terminator as your bodyguard against an evil snowman invasion?

Would you rather...

*Decorate an 80 ft tall gingerbread man **OR** bake a 1 ton fruitcake?*

Would you rather...

*Give up gingerbread cookies **OR** eggnog?*

Would you rather...

*Have to write Santa's 'naughty or nice' list **OR** check the list twice for him?*

Would you rather...

*'Drive' a sleigh with Santa's reindeer **OR** drive a Lamborghini on Christmas day?*

Would you rather...

*Be able to control the temperature **OR***

be able to fly?

Would you rather...

*Get stuck in a chimney for 4 hours **OR***

wear ugly sweaters for 4 months?

Would you rather...

Always be 45 minutes early OR 10 minutes late?

Would you rather...

Solve global warming OR end world hunger?

Would you rather...

*Have eggnog flavored fruitcake **OR** fruit cake flavored eggnog?*

Would you rather...

*Give up texting **OR** calling?*

Would you rather...

*Be able to tell if someone is lying **OR***

always get away with a lie?

Would you rather...

*Be famous **OR** powerful?*

Would you rather...

*Have an oversized head **OR** a very high pitched voice?*

Would you rather...

*Sound like Jar-Jar Binks from Star Wars **OR** Siri?*

Would you rather...

*Have a carrot for a nose **OR** reindeer hoof hands?*

Would you rather...

*Have your breath come out as Darth Vader's **OR** your voice come out as Yoda's?*

Would you rather...

Have uncontrollable sneezing OR

uncontrollable farting?

Would you rather...

Have the ability to freeze time OR

travel in time?

Would you rather...

*Not be able to listen to music **OR** not watch TV?*

Would you rather...

lose all of your luggage or lose all the gifts you bought at the airport?

Would you rather...

*Find your true love **OR** have your*

dream job?

Would you rather...

Be trapped in a room with 100 spiders

*for a day **OR** eat 3 spiders?*

Would you rather...

spend an entire day untangling Christmas lights **OR** spend an entire day overcooking Christmas cookies?

Would you rather...

Have skis for feet **OR** tinsel for hair?

Would you rather...

Vacation in the mountains **OR** on the beach?

Would you rather...

Be permanently covered head to toe in fur **OR** have antlers that fall off and grow back every year?

Would you rather...

*Knit a sweater made of Santa's beard hair **OR** wear a sweater made of Santa's beard hair?*

Would you rather...

*Invent a new gadget **OR** discover a new scientific theory?*

Would you rather...

*Have smelly feet **OR** bad breath?*

Would you rather...

*Eat a candy cane sandwich **OR** walk around the mall with mistletoe over your head for **2** hours?*

Would you rather...

*Read a book **OR** watch a movie of the book?*

Would you rather...

*Be Batman **OR** Ironman?*

Would you rather...

*Be Bruce Wayne **OR** Tony Stark?*

Would you rather...

*Have a big belly like Santa Claus **OR***

have a big glowing red nose like

Rudolph?

Would you rather...

Have 11 pipers piping **OR** 12 drummers drumming?

Would you rather...

Be completely alone **OR** have 100 people crammed into your house all Christmas day?

Would you rather...

*Clean the floor with a toothbrush **OR***

mow the lawn with scissors?

Would you rather...

*Get accidentally locked in the mall **OR***

stuck at the airport on Christmas?

Would you rather...

*Have candy canes for fingers **OR***

gumdrops for eyes?

Would you rather...

*Have the ability to fly **OR** read minds?*

Would you rather...

Read a 2,000-page book about Christmas **OR** write a 2,000-page book about Christmas?

Would you rather...

Be a superhero **OR** a wizard?

Would you rather...

*Fall into a puddle of mud **OR** into a pile of yellow snow?*

Would you rather...

*Do 100 pushups **OR** 100 situps?*

Would you rather...

*Be a famous actor **OR** a famous athlete?*

Would you rather...

*Shop for 2,000 gifts **OR** wrap 2,000 gifts?*

Would you rather...

*Get yelled at by Mom **OR** Dad?*

Would you rather...

*Only be awake at night **OR** during the day for Christmas?*

Would you rather...

*Eat pizza for the rest of your life **OR** burgers?*

Would you rather...

*Only be able to eat breakfast **OR** dinner forever?*

Would you rather...

Celebrate Christmas every month OR

once every 10 years?

Would you rather...

Have a runny nose OR a stuffy nose?

Would you rather...

Never have to do homework again **OR**

be paid to do your homework?

Would you rather...

Be really cold **OR** *really hot?*

Would you rather...

Sing Christmas songs solo to an audience of 2 million people **OR** wet your pants while sitting on Santa's lap?

Would you rather...

Have elf ears **OR** Santa's white beard forever?

Would you rather...

Have Santa Claus sneeze in your face or have a reindeer poop on your shoes?

Would you rather...

*Be super fast **OR** super strong?*

Would you rather...

*Stay up very late **OR** wake up very early?*

Would you rather...

*Never have to do homework again **OR** never take a test again?*

Would you rather...

Have holiday decorations up all year
OR *never be able to put them up?*

Would you rather...

Have a dinosaur **OR** *a dragon as a pet?*

Would you rather...

*Only be able to speak in Christmas song lyrics **OR** only be able to speak in Christmas movie quotes?*

Would you rather...

*Travel back in time **OR** to the future?*

Would you rather...

*Spend 2 days cooking a giant Christmas meal **OR** 2 days cleaning up after the Christmas meal?*

Would you rather...

*Be Santa **OR** Rudolph?*

Would you rather...

Never eat candy **OR** never play in the snow again?

Would you rather...

Always talk in riddles **OR** sing whenever you speak?

Would you rather...

*Wear clown makeup for 6 months straight **OR** a pink tutu?*

Would you rather...

*Always have a booger showing in your nose **OR** food stuck in your teeth?*

Would you rather...

Eat cookies **OR** cake?

Would you rather...

Be the most popular kid in school **OR** the smartest?

Would you rather...

Play inside all day **OR** outside?

Would you rather...

Have to set the table before dinner **OR**
clean up after?

Would you rather...

*Live in **Narnia OR** in Hogwarts?*

Would you rather...

*Not use your phone **OR** computer for a month?*

Would you rather...

*Ski **OR** snowboard?*

Would you rather...

*Have only 3 close friends **OR** many*

acquaintances?

Would you rather...

Be forced to listen to music all the time OR never listen to it?

Would you rather...

Give one person a $1,000 OR give 1,000 people a $1 gift?

Would you rather...

Eat a Christmas dinner covered in cranberry sauce **OR** gravy?

Would you rather...

Never have hot chocolate again **OR** never watch a Christmas movie ever again?

Would you rather...

Live in a giant gingerbread mansion **OR** build one?

Would you rather...

Be a genius in a world of idiots **OR** an idiot in a world of geniuses?

Would you rather...

Accidentally pee your pants in public
OR *not brush your teeth for a week?*

Would you rather...

Chug a gallon of eggnog in 15 seconds
OR *eat 80 sugar cookies in 15 minutes?*

Would you rather...

Have your clothes be 2 sizes too small **OR** 2 sizes too big?

Would you rather...

Not be able to taste **OR** smell?

Enjoying the book so far? Let us know what you think by leaving a review!

What has been your favorite question from the book thus far?

Would you rather...

*Be one of Santa's elves **OR** reindeer?*

Would you rather...

*Spend a day with you favorite fictional character **OR** favorite celebrity?*

Would you rather...

*Eat rotten eggs **OR** drink rotten milk?*

Would you rather...

*Get many small presents for Christmas **OR** one big one?*

Would you rather...

Spend a day watching Christmas movies OR shopping at the mall?

Would you rather...

Receive socks OR a dictionary for Christmas?

Would you rather...

Live in a giant gingerbread house **OR**
ride on the Polar Express?

Would you rather...

Eat your cereal with eggnog instead of
milk **OR** eat a candy cane sandwich?

Would you rather...

*Have Christmas tree tinsel for hair **OR** nails that light up like Christmas?*

Would you rather...

*Be at home on Christmas and get lots of presents **OR** be at Disneyland but get no presents?*

Would you rather...

*Have a rock chip in your shoe **OR** a hair in your eye?*

Would you rather...

*Own a Mercedes Benz **OR** a BMW?*

Would you rather...

Have Frosty as your friend **OR**

Rudolph?

Would you rather...

Drive a Lamborghini **OR** Ferrari?

Would you rather...

Not celebrate your birthday **OR** Christmas?

Would you rather...

Work at McDonalds **OR** Burger King?

Would you rather...

*Work at Walmart **OR** McDonalds for a year?*

Would you rather...

*Eat a whole turkey in one sitting **OR** never be able to eat turkey again?*

Would you rather...

Get the best gift you ever received

*again **OR** take a chance on a new gift?*

Would you rather...

*Celebrate Christmas **OR** New Years?*

Would you rather...

Would you rather spend the holidays with your family OR with three celebrities

Would you rather...

Eat Indian food OR Mexican food?

Would you rather...

*Get a papercut every time you touched paper **OR** bite your tongue every time you ate food?*

Would you rather...

*Be able to teleport **OR** read minds?*

Would you rather...

*Wear your grandma's clothes **OR** have her hairstyle?*

Would you rather...

*Be famous for starring in a cheesy holiday movie **OR** not be famous at all?*

Would you rather...

*Lose the ability to lie **OR** believe everything you hear to be true?*

Would you rather...

*Hear the good news **OR** bad news first?*

Would you rather...

*Be the villain **OR** the hero in a movie?*

Would you rather...

*Work untangling Christmas lights **OR** work as a mall Santa?*

Would you rather...

*Be 4'0 **OR** 8'0?*

Would you rather...

*Be in constant pain **OR** have a constant itch?*

Would you rather...

*Give up Christmas trees **OR** Christmas cookies*

Would you rather...

*Use eyedrops made of lemon juice **OR** toilet paper made of sandpaper?*

Would you rather...

*Take a guaranteed $100,000 **OR** take a 50/50 chance at $500,000?*

Would you rather...

*Never be able to take a hot shower again **OR** never eat hot food again?*

Would you rather...

*Never play **OR** always play and never win?*

Would you rather...

*Know what all your gifts are **OR** be surprised by all your gifts?*

Would you rather...

*Be a chronic farter **OR** a chronic burper?*

Would you rather...

*Only have dessert on holidays **OR** never have dessert on holidays*

Would you rather...

Never use an electronic device ever again **OR** *never talk to a human again?*

Would you rather...

Be a vegetarian **OR** *only be able to eat meat?*

Would you rather...

*Have **2** wishes today **OR 3** wishes in 10 years?*

Would you rather...

*Go to a big party **OR** a small get together for the holidays?*

Would you rather...

*Eat a stick of butter **OR** a teaspoon of cinnamon?*

Would you rather...

*Sing Jingle Bells non-stop for 24 hours **OR** not celebrate Christmas this year?*

Would you rather...

Have no Winter Break OR Spring Break?

Would you rather...

Be able to eat as much junk food as you want and not get fat OR receive a million dollars?

Would you rather...

*Be able to see your own future **OR***

other people's futures and not yours?

Would you rather...

*Never remember faces **OR** names?*

Would you rather...

*Win a gingerbread house-building contest **OR** a cookie-baking contest?*

Would you rather...

*Get a useful gift **OR** a fun gift?*

Would you rather...

Star on a popular holiday music single
OR *in a popular holiday movie??*

Would you rather...

Vacation somewhere cold OR hot
during the holidays?

Would you rather...

Give up the internet for a month **OR** transportation?

Would you rather...

Be homeless **OR** have no friends?

Would you rather...

*Have your team mascot be a turkey **OR** a reindeer?*

Would you rather...

*Not be able to ask questions **OR** give answers?*

Would you rather...

*Have a snow week off from school **OR** an extra week of summer vacation?*

Would you rather...

*Be rich and ugly **OR** poor and good looking?*

Would you rather...

Wear winter clothes in the Sahara **OR**

no clothes in the Arctic?

Would you rather...

Have all your presents wrapped

terribly **OR** *not wrapped at all?*

Thank you for reading! If you enjoyed the book, leave us a review and let us know what you liked or what you would like to see next.

As a special bonus, enjoy this exclusive preview of one our other popular titles!

Try Not To Laugh

Challenge

Christmas Edition

Joke Book

How To Play

Step 1

Split into two teams whether that be boys vs girls, kids vs parents, or any mix of your choice. If possible, also assign one person as a referee. You can also do 1 vs 1!

Step 2

Decide who gets to go first. Which team can do the most pushups? Which team can guess the number between 1 and 10 from someone not playing the game? Or just a good old fashioned rock paper scissors?

Step 3

The starting team has to tell a joke from the book. You can say the joke however you like and animate it too with funny faces, gestures, voices or whatever else!

Step 4

If everyone on the opposing team laughs, the other team gets a point! Set a limit for how many points it takes to win and the first team to reach the limit, wins!

What language does Santa speak?

North Polish

What do reindeer say before telling their best jokes?

This will sleigh you!

Who is a Christmas tree's favorite singer?

Spruce Springsteen

What's red and white and keeps falling down chimneys?

Santa Klutz

Where do Christmas plants go to become movie stars?

Holly-wood

How does a cow like to say Merry Christmas?

Moowy Christmas

What do you get when you cross Christmas and a duck?

Christmas quackers

What falls in the winter but never gets hurt?

Snow!

What is the ratio of a pumpkin's circumference to its diameter?

Pumpkin Pi

What's the key to a great Christmas dinner?

The turKE

If you enjoyed this title, check out our other books by searching "Hayden Fox" on Amazon!